Ohio State Buckeyes Football

Progressive Trivia

Researched by Paul F. Wilson

Paul F. Wilson & Tom P. Rippey III, Editors

Kick The Ball, Ltd

Lewis Center, Ohio

Progressive Trivia Books

by Kick The Ball, Ltd

Professional Baseball

Boston Red Sox

New York Yankees

St. Louis Cardinals

Professional Football

Green Bay Packers

New York Giants

Pittsburgh Steelers

College Football

Ohio State Buckeyes

Ohio State Buckeyes Football: Progressive Trivia;
First Edition 2012

Published by
Kick The Ball, Ltd
8595 Columbus Pike, Suite 197
Lewis Center, OH 43035
www.ProgressiveTriviaBooks.com

Edited by: Paul F. Wilson & Tom P. Rippey III
Designed and Formatted by Paul F. Wilson
Researched by: Paul F. Wilson

International Standard Book Number: 978-1-61320-056-8

Printed and Bound in the United States of America

10 9 8 7 6 5 4 3 2 1

Table of Contents

About
Progressive Trivia Books
by Kick The Ball, Ltd

Play ***Ohio State Buckeyes Football: Progressive Trivia*** by yourself or with others, either way we hope you enjoy playing.

Each page of this book presents six questions that relate in some way to one another. Likewise, each question progresses through that page's theme in a way that builds on the previous question's answer, or the previous question itself. In so doing, a more complete picture emerges about the subject matter of that set of six questions.

Questions can take the form of: multiple choice; true or false; yes or no; fill in the blank; or simply a question with no answer options at all. Each type of question challenges you in a unique way to test your knowledge of the team's history, great moments, traditions, key players and coaches, championships, individual and team records, and much more.

The answers to each set of questions are conveniently placed at the bottom of that page. You may want to *cover the answers prior to beginning a section* to avoid prematurily revealing an answer to yourself.

Although we have taken care to avoid errors in this book, from time to time they may occur. If you find one, we ask for your understanding and thank you for bringing it to our attention. Please email tprippey@progressivetriviabooks.com with any comments or observations. Thank you and we sincerely hope you enjoy playing ***Ohio State Buckeyes Football: Progressive Trivia.***

All information in this book is valid as of the end of the 2011 season.

Ohio State Buckeyes Football

1) Who is the Buckeyes' all-time leading passer?

2) How many total passing yards did he have?

3) Did he have more career touchdown passes than interceptions?

4) How many career pass completions did he amass?

A) 397
B) 437
C) 467
D) 497

5) What years did he play for the Buckeyes?

6) Did he have fewer or more than 1,000 career passing attempts?

Reminder: A question may refer to the previous question on the same page.

Answers:

1) Art Schlichter
2) 7,547
3) Yes; 50 TDs to 46 INTs
4) D – 497
5) 1978-81
6) Fewer; 951

7) Who was the Buckeyes' most recent Rose Bowl Player of the Game?

8) How many times have Buckeyes been named Rose Bowl Player of the Game?

9) The team's first Rose Bowl Player of the Game award was given to a Buckeye in ______.

10) Where does Ohio State rank in its all-time number of Rose Bowl Player of the Game awards compared to other teams?

11) In how many of their Rose Bowl appearances did a Buckeye not win a Player of the Game award?

12) Joe Germaine had 131 passing yards en route to winning a Rose Bowl Player of the Game award against which team?

Answers:

7) Terrelle Pryor; 2010
8) Six
9) 1950; Fred "Curly" Morrison
10) Fourth; Ohio State, Oregon and UCLA each have six.
11) Eight; One was prior to the creation of the award in 1953
12) Arizona State; Ohio State 20, Arizona State 17

13) When was the ground breaking for Ohio Stadium?

14) What was the stadium's original cost of construction?

15) What is the stadium's current seating capacity?

16) Who owns the stadium?

17) Who is the Buckeyes' co-tenant at the stadium?

18) The stadium's playing surface is artificial turf.

A) True
B) False

Answers:

13) Aug. 3, 1921
14) $1.34 million
15) 102,329
16) The Ohio State University
17) No current co-tenant
18) A – True; FieldTurf since 2007

19) What year did Ohio State's Athletic Council officially adopt the name Buckeyes for the university's athletic teams?

20) A ____________ is awarded to football players for outstanding team plays.

21) Is Aesculus glabra the binomial name of the Ohio Buckeye tree?

22) The seed of the Aesculus glabra is said to resemble what?

23) Were Ohio State's school colors ever officially chestnut brown?

24) Carrying a buckeye in one's pocket is said to:

A) Repel vampires
B) Attract a mate
C) Bring good luck
D) Cure the common cold

Answers:

19) 1950
20) Buckeye leaf
21) Yes
22) The eye of a buck, or male deer
23) No; They were almost orange and black, however.
24) C – Bring good luck; Also rumored to relieve rheumatism

25) Did Ohio State football players wear head protection in 1890?

26) The Buckeyes' 1942 National Championship team wore leather helmets.

A) True
B) False

27) What color were Ohio State's helmets in 1942?

28) Did Buckeye helmets have a facemask in 1954?

29) Were Buckeye helmets ever black?

30) Current Ohio State helmets are relatively unchanged since their introduction in what year?

Answers:

25) No; They wore a red and white striped hat.
26) A – True
27) Scarlet
28) No
29) No
30) 1968

31) There are a total of 20 Ohio State Buckeyes players and coaches in the College Football Hall of Fame.

A) True
B) False

32) What year was the first Buckeye inducted into the College Football Hall of Fame?

33) How many Buckeyes were members of the College Football Hall of Fame's charter class?

34) Which of the following represented the Buckeyes in the charter class of the College Football Hall of Fame?

A) John Wilce and Wes Fesler
B) Les Horvath and Francis Schmidt
C) Bill Willis and Gaylord Stinchcomb
D) Chic Harley and Howard Jones

35) Woody Hayes was a member of which class?

36) Who was the most recent Buckeye player to be inducted into the College Football Hall of Fame?

Answers:

31) B – False; 29 players and coaches
32) 1951
33) Two
34) D – Chic Harley and Howard Jones
35) 1983
36) Eddie George; Class of 2011

37) How many Buckeyes were drafted in the 2012 NFL Draft?

38) How many of these Buckeyes were selected in the first round?

39) Who was the first Buckeye selected in the 2012 NFL Draft?

A) DeVier Posey
B) Mike Adams
C) Dan Herron
D) Nate Ebner

40) In which round was he taken?

41) Which team selected him?

42) Who was the final Buckeye taken in the 2012 NFL Draft?

Answers:

37) Four
38) Zero
39) B – Mike Adams
40) Second
41) Pittsburgh Steelers
42) Nate Ebner; Pick 27 of Round Six

43) The Buckeyes have made _____ all-time appearances in BCS Bowl games?

44) Which other FBS team has made the same number of BCS Bowl appearances as Ohio State?

45) What year did the Buckeyes play in their first-ever BCS Bowl game?

46) Did the Buckeyes travel to Atlanta, Ga., to play in the 1999 Sugar Bowl?

A) Yes
B) No

47) What is the Buckeyes' winning percentage in BCS Bowl games?

48) How many BCS National Championships has Ohio State won?

Answers:

43) Nine
44) None; Oklahoma is closest with eight.
45) 1999
46) B – No; New Orleans, La.
47) .667; 6-3 all-time record
48) One; 2002 Fiesta Bowl

49) Mike Vrabel is the Buckeyes' all-time sacks leader.

A) True
B) False

50) How many sacks did he have?

51) How many seasons did he play at Ohio State?

52) Who is second on the all-time career sacks leaders list, Matt Finkes or Jason Simmons?

53) How many career sacks does the No. 2 player on the list have?

54) Do any current Buckeyes rank in the top five of the team's all-time sacks leaders list?

A) Yes
B) No

Answers:

49) A – True
50) 36.0
51) Four; 1993-96
52) Jason Simmons
53) 27.5
54) B – No

55) How many jersey numbers have the Buckeyes officially retired?

56) Who wore the jersey number which was retired in 1999?

57) What jersey number did he wear at Ohio State?

58) Which Buckeye was allowed to wear that number from 1996-98?

59) Whose jersey number was most recently retired?

60) Who is the only Heisman trophy winner at Ohio State without a retired jersey number?

Answers:

55) Eight; Includes "WH" retired for Woody Hayes in 2005
56) Archie Griffin
57) No. 45
58) Andy Katzenmoyer
59) Bill Willis; 2007
60) Troy Smith

61) The 2003 Fiesta Bowl between the Buckeyes and the Miami Hurricanes was played in the city of ______________.

62) What was the name of the host stadium for the game?

63) What was the final score of the game?

64) Who was favored heading into the game and by how much?

65) How many overtimes were played that game?

66) Who were the game's MVPs?

Answers:

61) Tempe, Ariz.
62) Sun Devil Stadium
63) Ohio State 31, Miami (Fla.) 24
64) Miami, 11.5 points
65) Two
66) Craig Krenzel and Mike Doss

67) Who owns the Buckeyes' record for the most career receiving touchdowns?

68) How many receiving touchdowns did he have?

A) 34
B) 44
C) 48
D) 52

69) How many seasons was he a starter at Ohio State?

70) When was his first season with the team?

71) Which team drafted him in the 1999 NFL Draft?

72) Is he originally from Arizona?

Answers:

67) David Boston
68) A – 34
69) Three
70) 1996; Through 1998
71) Arizona Cardinals; Round One, Pick Eight
72) No; Texas

73) When was the Buckeyes' record for the longest-ever field goal made set?

74) Who successfully kicked the field goal?

75) How many yards was the record-setting field goal?

76) Where was the record set?

A) Purdue
B) Michigan
C) Wisconsin
D) Illinois

77) Was the record-setting field goal also the game-winning field goal that day?

A) Yes
B) No

78) Does he also own the Buckeyes' record for the longest field goal in Ohio Stadium?

Answers:

73) 1975
74) Tom Skladany
75) 59
76) D – Illinois
77) B – No; No. 1 Ohio State 40, Illinois 3
78) No; Mike Nugent 55 yards vs. Marshall, 2004

79) Who holds the Buckeyes' record for the highest single-season passing completion percentage (min. 250 attempts)?

80) When did he set the team record in the category?

81) What was his record completion percentage that season?

82) He completed _____ of _____ passes that year.

83) How many games did he play that season?

84) He is also second on the team's list for the highest passing completion percentage in a season.

A) True
B) False

Answers:

79) Troy Smith
80) 2006
81) .653
82) 203, 311
83) 12
84) B – False; Terrelle Pryor, .650 in 2010

85) The Buckeyes' record for the most career touchdown passes is owned by which quarterbacks?

A) Mike Tomczak and Greg Frey
B) Joe Germaine and Jim Karsatos
C) Troy Smith and Art Schlichter
D) Terrelle Pryor and Bobby Hoying

86) How many career touchdown passes did they complete?

87) How many seasons did it take to accumulate their record-setting career touchdown passes?

88) Which years did they spend with the Buckeyes?

89) Their individual career totals in the category are twice as high as the next highest Buckeye QB on the list.

A) True
B) False

90) Does Craig Krenzel appear in the top-10 list for this category?

Answers:

85) D – Terrelle Pryor and Bobby Hoying
86) 57
87) Three (Terrelle Pryor) and Four (Bobby Hoying)
88) 2008-10 (Terrelle Pryor) and 1992-95 (Bobby Hoying)
89) B – False; No. 3 Joe Germaine has 56.
90) No

91) What is the Buckeyes' record for the most punt returns by a player in a single game?

92) Who set the record?

93) Against what team was the record set?

94) What year did he set the team record?

95) How many punt return yards did he have that game?

A) 58
B) 64
C) 71
D) 76

96) Did his punt returns that day help him set the Buckeyes' single-season record in the category as well?

Answers:

91) Nine
92) Tom Campana
93) Indiana Hoosiers
94) 1971
95) D – 76
96) No; He is sixth on that list with his performance in 1971.

97) Eddie George holds the Buckeyes' career record for the most 100-yard rushing games.

A) True
B) False

98) How many 100-yard rushing games does the career leader have?

99) When was his first season with the team?

100) When was his final season with the team?

101) How many 100-yard rushing games did Eddie George have during his career at Ohio State?

102) Who is third on the Buckeyes' list for the category and how many 100-yard rushing games did he have?

Answers:

97) B – False; Archie Griffin
98) 34
99) 1972
100) 1975
101) 20
102) Chris "Beanie" Wells and Keith Byars, 17 each

103) Who was the Buckeyes' opponent in the 2012 Gator Bowl?

104) In which city was the game played?

105) The Buckeyes were defeated by their 2012 Gator Bowl rival by 14 points.

A) True
B) False

106) Who was named the game's MVP?

107) Did the game's MVP set a Gator Bowl record with a 99-yard kick return?

108) How much did each team receive for their appearance in the game?

Answers:

103) Florida Gators
104) Jacksonville, Fla.
105) B – False; Florida 24, Ohio State 17
106) Andre Debose, Florida
107) Yes
108) $2.5 million

109) How many yards is the longest interception return in Buckeyes history?

110) Who holds the Buckeyes' all-time record for the longest interception return?

111) When was the team record set?

112) Against which team was the interception returned?

113) How many yards is the second-longest interception return in Buckeyes history?

114) Who holds the record for the second-longest interception return?

A) Howard Cassady
B) Ed Thompson
C) Kurt Coleman
D) Ed Thompson

Answers:

109) 100 yards
110) Will Allen, Marlon Kerner and David Brown
111) W. Allen (2003), M. Kerner (1993) and D. Brown (1986)
112) W. Allen (San Diego State), M. Kerner (Purdue) and D. Brown (Purdue)
113) 89
114) C – Kurt Coleman

115) The Buckeyes' single-game rushing yards record was set versus Illinois.

A) True
B) False

116) Who set the record versus Illinois that day?

117) When was the record in the category set?

118) How many carries did he have that game?

119) Did any of his rushing attempts result in a touchdown?

120) Did the Buckeyes win the ball game as a result of his record-setting performance?

Answers:

115) A – True; 314 yards
116) Eddie George
117) 1995
118) 36
119) Yes; Two
120) Yes; Ohio State 41, Illinois 3

121) David Boston shares the Buckeyes' record for the most 100-yard receiving games in a season with whom?

A) Cris Carter
B) Terry Glenn
C) Michael Jenkins
D) No co-holder for this record

122) How many 100-yard receiving games in a season did he have to set the team record?

123) What year did he have his record-setting season?

124) David Boston had four or more 100-yard receiving games in a season two times.

A) True
B) False

125) Terry Glenn had ___ 100-yard receiving games in 1995.

126) Cris Carter is the only other Buckeye to have five or more 100-yard receiving games in a single season?

Answers:

121) D – No co-holder for this record
122) Nine
123) 1998
124) A – True; Nine (1998) and Four (1997)
125) Seven
126) True; Five in 1986

127) What are the most games the Buckeyes have ever won in a single season?

128) What year did the Buckeyes win the most games in school history?

129) Did the Buckeyes win 19 straight games from 2002-03?

130) Which team ended the Buckeyes' consecutive wins streak in 2003?

131) What is Ohio State's all-time longest winning streak (without ties)?

132) When was that team record set?

Answers:

127) 14
128) 2002
129) Yes; 14 games in 2002 and five games in 2003
130) Wisconsin
131) 22 games
132) 1967-69

133) ______________ was the most recent Buckeye to score five touchdowns in a single game.

134) What season did he set this mark?

135) Against which team did he score the four TDs?

136) Who is the only other Buckeye to score five TDs in a single game?

137) What season did he accomplish the feat?

138) Against which team did he accomplish the feat?

Answers:

133) Keith Byars
134) 1984
135) Illinois
136) Pete Johnson
137) 1975
138) North Carolina

139) What is the Buckeyes' team record for the most fumbles lost in a single season?

140) How many total fumbles did they have that season?

141) What season did this occur?

142) What was Ohio State's record that season?

143) The Buckeyes' record for the fewest fumbles lost in a season is three.

A) True
B) False

144) What season was the team record for the fewest fumbles lost set?

Answers:

139) 21
140) 34
141) 1951
142) 4-3-2
143) False; Two of nine fumbles were lost.
144) 2010

145) What year was Wayne Woodrow Hayes born?

146) He was born in the state of _______?

147) Which college did he attend?

148) Which position did he play in college?

A) Tackle
B) Guard
C) Center
D) Tight End

149) What was his nickname?

150) He coached at Miami (Fla.) just prior to coaching at Ohio State?

A) True
B) False

Answers:

145) 1913
146) Ohio
147) Denison
148) A – Tackle
149) Woody
150) B – False; Miami (Ohio)

151) Which Buckeye holds the team's record for the most career points scored?

152) How many career points did he score?

153) He played for the Buckeyes from 2001-______.

154) How many points after touchdown did he record?

155) How many field goals did he make?

156) He was a consensus All-American twice while at Ohio State.

A) True
B) False

Answers:

151) Mike Nugent
152) 356
153) 2004
154) 140
155) 72
156) A – True; 2002 and 2004

157) The Buckeyes' career record for the most all-purpose yards is held by ______________.

158) How many total all-purpose yards did he have?

159) How many career games did he play as a Buckeye?

A) 40
B) 45
C) 50
D) 55

160) Was his career total all-purpose yards greater than Carlos Snow's and Tim Spencer's combined?

161) Who is ranked second on the career leaders list for this category?

162) How many total all-purpose yards does the No. 2 player on the list have?

Answers:

157) Archie Griffin
158) 6,559
159) B – 45
160) No; They combined for 9,453 career all-purpose yards.
161) Carlos Snow
162) 4,851

163) Where did the Buckeyes set the team record for the most points scored in a game?

A) Home
B) Away

164) What team was visiting the Buckeyes that day?

165) What year was the game played?

166) How many points did the Buckeyes score that game?

167) Since 1950, what are the most points the Buckeyes have scored in a single game?

168) Against which team did they accomplish this feat?

Answers:

163) A – Home
164) Oberlin
165) 1916
166) 128
167) 83
168) Iowa

169) Who holds the Buckeyes' record for the most passes had intercepted in a game?

A) Rex Kern
B) Art Schlichter
C) Ron Maciejowski
D) Greg Frey

170) Which team intercepted the passes?

171) How many passes did they intercept?

172) How many passing attempts did he have on the day?

173) How many passing touchdowns did he have?

174) Despite the interceptions, he still managed to pass for more than 200 yards that game.

A) True
B) False

Answers:

169) B – Art Schlichter
170) Penn State
171) Five
172) 26
173) Zero
174) B – False; 182 yards

175) The Buckeyes' career record for the most consecutive points after touchdown made is over 100.

A) True
B) False

176) Who holds the team record in the category?

177) When did the streak begin?

178) When did the streak end?

179) Who holds the No. 2 spot on Ohio State's career list for this category?

180) How many consecutive points after touchdown did he make?

Answers:

175) False; 86
176) Tim Williams
177) 1991
178) 1993
179) Mike Nugent
180) 83

181) All time, how many times have Buckeyes been selected to the Senior Bowl?

182) How many Buckeyes were selected to the Senior Bowl in 1950, the inaugural Senior Bowl?

183) What is the highest number of Buckeyes to be selected to the Senior Bowl in a year?

184) What year were the most Buckeyes selected for the game?

185) In the year the most Buckeyes were selected for the game, which players were selected?

186) Since 2000, which season did no Buckeye get selected for the Senior Bowl?

Answers:

181) 71
182) Zero
183) Six
184) 2004
185) Will Allen, Tim Anderson, Adrien Clarke, Michael Jenkins, Shane Olivea and Alex Stepanovich
186) 2001

187) What is the distance of the longest-ever punt in Buckeyes history?

A) 74 yards
B) 78 yards
C) 83 yards
D) 87 yards

188) The Buckeyes' longest punt was kicked by __________.

189) Ohio State was visiting which team the day he kicked the record-setting punt?

190) What year did he set the record?

191) Did Gary Lago and Howard Wedebrook both kick 80-yard punts for the Buckeyes?

192) What year did Gary Lago kick his 80-yarder?

Answers:

187) D – 87 yards
188) Karl Edwards
189) Illinois
190) 1983
191) No; H. Wedebrook's longest was 78 yards, 1936.
192) 1972; at Michigan State

193) Did Rich Spangler kick more points after touchdown in his career as a Buckeye than Vlade Janakievski?

194) Who kicked the third-most points after touchdown in Buckeyes history?

195) How many PATs did he kick?

196) How many seasons was he at Ohio State?

197) Did Vlade Janakievski have more PAT attempts in his career as a Buckeye than Rich Spangler?

198) How many total career PAT attempts separate the two kickers?

Answers:

193) Yes; R. Spangler (177) and V. Janakievski (172)
194) Dan Stultz
195) 165
196) Four; 1997-2000
197) No
198) Five; R. Spangler (184) and V. Janakievski (179)

199) What is Ohio State's team record for the most touchdowns in a single game?

200) Against which opponent did they accomplish this feat?

201) Where was this game played?

A) Home
B) Away

202) What is Ohio State's team record for the most touchdowns allowed in a game?

203) Which teams hold this record?

204) Where was this game played?

A) Home
B) Away

Answers:

199) 19
200) Oberlin
201) A – Home
202) 15
203) Michigan
204) B – Away; Ann Arbor, Mich.

205) Who was the Buckeyes' opponent in the 1971 Rose Bowl?

206) Where is the Rose Bowl located?

207) What was Ohio State's record heading into the game?

208) What was Ohio State's AP ranking heading into the game?

209) What was the name of the opposing quarterback?

210) Despite a 27-17 Rose Bowl loss that day, was Ohio State still named 1970 National Champions by the NFF?

Answers:

205) Stanford Indians
206) Pasadena, Calif.
207) 9-0
208) No. 2
209) Jim Plunkett
210) Yes

211) ______________ holds the Buckeyes' record for the most punt returns in a season.

212) What year did he set the team record for the category?

213) How many punt returns did he have that season?

214) Who holds the No. 2 spot on the list for the category?

215) How many punts did the No. 2 player return in a season to earn his place on the list?

216) What year was the No. 2 spot secured?

A) 1970
B) 1971
C) 1973
D) 1975

Answers:

211) David Boston
212) 1997
213) 47
214) Neal Colzie
215) 40
216) C – 1973

217) Who founded the “Pants Club” at Ohio State?

218) What year did he found it?

219) What do the gold pants charms represent?

220) What famous quote by the Pants Club founder led to the gold pants charms?

221) What relationship did the founder have with the Buckeyes?

A) Head Coach
B) Athletic Director
C) Team Physician
D) Player

222) What is inscribed on the gold pants charms?

Answers:

217) Francis Schmidt
218) 1934
219) A victory over Michigan
220) "They [Michigan Wolverines] put their pants on one leg at a time just like everybody else.”
221) A – Head Coach; 1934-40
222) Recipient’s initials, the year and score of the game

223) Who owns the Buckeyes' record for the most career interceptions?

224) How many career interceptions did he have?

225) He played for the Buckeyes from 1968 through ______.

226) Does William White have one fewer career interception than Fred Bruney?

227) How many career interceptions does Fred Bruney have?

228) How many seasons did it take him to accumulate his second-best number of interceptions?

Answers:

223) Mike Sensibaugh
224) 22
225) 1970
226) Yes
227) 17
228) Three; 1950-52

229) Terry Glenn set the Buckeyes' record for the most yards receiving in a season.

A) True
B) False

230) What is the Buckeyes' record for the most yards receiving in a season?

231) When was the record set?

232) How many times does Cris Carter appear in the top 10 spots of the list for this category?

233) Who holds the No. 2 spot on the list?

234) He had ________ yards receiving in the _______ season.

Answers:

229) B – False; David Boston
230) 1,435
231) 1998
232) Two; Nos. 3 and 8
233) Terry Glenn
234) 1,411, 1995

235) What is the Buckeyes' record for the most punt attempts in a single game?

236) Who holds the record?

237) Against what team was the record set?

238) What year was the record set?

239) A.J. Trapasso punted 11 times in two separate games in his career.

A) True
B) False

240) Who played more seasons with the Buckeyes, Vic Janowicz or A.J. Trapasso?

Answers:

235) 21
236) Vic Janowicz
237) Michigan
238) 1950
239) B – False; Once at Michigan in 2007
240) A.J. Trapasso; 4 seasons (2005-08) to 3 (1949-51)

241) What seasons did legendary Pittsburgh Steelers defensive coordinator Dick LeBeau play at OSU?

242) Dick LeBeau was selected to play in the Blue Gray All Star Football Classic in ______.

243) What position did LeBeau play while at Ohio State?

244) Ohio State won a National Championship in which of LeBeau's seasons in Columbus?

245) Which team drafted him in the 1959 NFL Draft?

246) What year was he enshrined into the Pro Football Hall of Fame?

Answers:

241) 1956-58
242) 1958
243) Cornerback
244) 1957
245) Cleveland Browns; Round Five, Pick 58
246) 2010

247) Has any Buckeye ever returned a kick for greater than 100 yards?

248) Who holds the Buckeyes' record for the longest-ever kick return?

249) What year did he set the team record for the category?

250) What opposing team was on the wrong side of his record-setting kick return?

251) Who is the most recent Buckeye to return a kickoff 100 yards?

252) What year and against which team did he make the return?

Answers:

247) Yes; Five times
248) Dean Sensanbaugher; 103 yards
249) 1943
250) Great Lakes
251) Ted Ginn, Jr.
252) 2005, Minnesota

253) What are the most penalties by the Buckeyes in a single game?

254) Did the penalties occur in a home or an away game?

255) The penalties resulted in a loss of _____ yards.

256) What was the outcome of that day's game?

257) Ohio State set its team record for the most penalty yards in a game in 2000.

A) True
B) False

258) Who was their opponent that game and how many yards were the Buckeyes penalized?

Answers:

253) 14
254) Home game
255) 120
256) Minnesota 57, Ohio State 3
257) A – True
258) Fresno State, 136

259) Does a running back or quarterback hold the Buckeyes' career record for the highest rushing average per attempt?

260) Who holds the record?

261) What was his career rushing average per attempt?

262) Who is second on the career list in the category?

263) What was his career rushing average?

264) Who is the highest ranked quarterback on the list?

Answers:

259) Running back
260) Archie Griffin
261) 6.0
262) Calvin Murray
263) 5.9
264) Terrelle Pryor; Ranked 15th with a 5.0 average

265) How many times has a Buckeye quarterback thrown five touchdown passes in a single game?

266) Which of the following Buckeyes QBs did not throw five TDs in a game?

A) John Borton
B) Troy Smith
C) Bobby Hoying
D) None of the above

267) When was the last time a Buckeye QB completed five TD passes in a single game?

268) Who was the Buckeyes' opponent that day?

269) When was the first time a Buckeye QB completed five TD passes in a single game?

270) Name the Buckeye quarterback who threw the five TD passes that day.

Answers:

265) Three
266) B – Troy Smith
267) 1995, Bobby Hoying
268) Pittsburgh
269) 1952
270) John Borton

271) Vernon Gholston owns the Buckeyes' record for the most quarterback sacks in a single season.

A) True
B) False

272) How many QB sacks make up the team record?

273) What season was the record set?

274) How many games did he play in that season?

275) __________ had the second most sacks that season.

276) How many sacks did the No. 2 players have?

Answers:

271) A – True
272) 14.0
273) 2007
274) 13
275) James Laurinaitis and Larry Grant
276) 5.0

277) How many career 100-yard receiving games did David Boston have?

278) Does David Boston or Michael Jenkins hold the Buckeyes' record in the category?

279) How many career games with 100-yards receiving did Michael Jenkins have?

280) Which of the above players spent the most seasons with the team?

281) Does any other Buckeye receiver have 10 or more career 100-yard games to his credit?

282) Who ranks third on the list and now many career 100-yard games did he have?

Answers:

277) 14
278) David Boston
279) 10
280) Tied, Both spent three seasons as a Buckeye
281) No
282) Cris Carter, Nine

283) A Buckeye kicker has made six field goals in a single game.

A) True
B) False

284) What is the Buckeyes' record in the category?

285) How many Buckeye kickers co-hold this record?

286) Name the four kickers who have accomplished this feat.

287) When was the most recent season this was accomplished?

288) Against which team was it accomplished?

Answers:

283) B – False
284) Five
285) Four
286) Devin Barclay, Josh Huston, Mike Nugent and Bob Atha
287) 2010
288) Miami (Fla.)

289) Who holds the Buckeyes' record for the most consecutive 100-yard rushing games in a season?

290) How many consecutive games did he rush for 100 or more yards during the streak?

291) What season did he set that mark?

292) Who is the only other Buckeye with 10 or more consecutive 100-yard rushing performances in a season?

293) How many seasons did he have 10 or more consecutive 100-yard rushing games?

294) Does he also own the NCAA record for the most consecutive 100-yard rushing games in a career?

Answers:

289) Eddie George
290) 12
291) 1995
292) Archie Griffin
293) Three; 1973-75
294) Yes, 31

295) What year was “The Best Damn Band in the Land” formed?

296) The band is comprised of how many members?

297) Are there any wood instruments in the band?

298) What is the band’s alternate nickname?

299) What is the name of the pre-game event that takes place in St. John Arena on game days in Columbus?

300) What is the band’s signature march known as?

Answers:

295) 1879
296) 225
297) No; All brass
298) “The Pride of the Buckeyes”
299) Skull Session
300) Script Ohio

301) What is the popular nickname for the Buckeyes' defense?

302) Which former OSU coach is credited with coining the term?

303) The 1996 Ohio State defense was the first to use the moniker.

A) True
B) False

304) Was current Buckeyes Assistant Head Coach Luke Fickell an original member of the Silver Bullets?

305) Which award did Andy Katzenmoyer, an original Silver Bullet, receive in 1997?

306) How many members of the 1996 Silver Bullets were drafted in the 1997 NFL Draft?

Answers:

301) Silver Bullets
302) Fred Pagac
303) A – True
304) Yes
305) Butkus Award
306) Five; Shawn Springs, Rob Kelly, Ty Howard, Mike Vrabel and Matt Finkes

307) Who holds the Buckeyes' record for the most career receptions?

308) How many career receptions does he have?

309) He accumulated his team-leading receptions from __________.

310) How many times was he named First Team All-Big Ten?

311) What year was he named First Team All-American?

312) His career-leading receptions also earned him the No. 3 spot on Ohio State's career list for receiving yards?

A) True
B) False

Answers:

307) David Boston
308) 191
309) 1996-98
310) Two; 1997 and 1998
311) 1998
312) B – False; No. 2 with 2,855 yards

313) Urban Meyer is the ____ all-time head coach of the Ohio State Buckeyes.

314) What year did Urban Meyer first coach at Ohio State as a graduate assistant?

315) How old was he when he was hired as the head coach of the Buckeyes?

316) Urban Meyer is the youngest-ever coach to win a National Championship in NCAA Division I football.

A) True
B) False

317) Including Urban Meyer, how many BCS head coaches have coached their teams to three 13-win seasons?

318) Which two news organizations named Urban Meyer the Coach of the Decade in December 2009?

Answers:

313) 24th
314) 1986
315) 47
316) B – False; Danny Ford, Clemson, 1981, Age of 33
317) One
318) *Sporting News* and *Sports Illustrated*

319) What year was the Buckeyes' record for the longest punt return set?

320) Against which team was the record set?

321) What Buckeyes return man set the record?

322) How many yards was his record-setting punt return?

323) Did he score a touchdown on the punt return?

324) Was he a part of any other scoring play that game?

Answers:

319) 2007
320) Kent State
321) Brian Hartline
322) 90
323) Yes
324) Yes; A 14-yard TD pass from Todd Boeckman

325) The Buckeyes played the ______________ in the 1955 Rose Bowl.

326) What was Ohio State's AP ranking entering the game?

327) Did Southern Cal have the AP's No. 2 ranking?

328) Why was UCLA unable to play in that year's Rose Bowl?

329) Ohio State defeated Southern Cal by how many points?

330) What were the results of the AP and Coaches polls following the game?

Answers:

325) Southern Cal Trojans
326) No. 1
327) No; UCLA was AP No. 2
328) Due to the "No-repeat" rule
329) 13
330) AP voted Ohio State and the Coaches voted UCLA for split National Champions.

331) Who co-holds the Buckeyes' record for the most points after touchdown made in a game?

A) Josh Jackson and Tom Klaban
B) Vlade Janakievski and Blair Conway
C) Devin Barclay and Vic Janowicz
D) Rich Spangler and Dan Stultz

332) How many extra points did they make to set the team record?

333) What years were their records set?

334) Against which teams were the records set?

335) Vlade Janakievski kicked nine PATs against which team twice?

336) Who is the only other Buckeye kicker to kick nine PATs in a single game?

Answers:

331) C – Devin Barclay and Vic Janowicz
332) 10
333) 1950 (Janowicz) and 2010 (Barclay)
334) Iowa (Janowicz) and Eastern Michigan (Barclay)
335) Northwestern; 1978 and 1980
336) Rich Spangler; 1983, Minnesota

337) How many Buckeyes have won the Heisman Memorial Trophy?

338) In addition to being the only two-time winner of the Heisman, Archie Griffin was also the first player to win it as a sophomore.

A) True
B) False

339) Who was Ohio State's first Heisman winner?

340) What season did he earn the honor?

341) Who became the Buckeyes' sixth Heisman winner in 2006?

342) How many Buckeyes have finished second in Heisman voting?

Answers:

337) Six; Of course one of them won it twice.
338) B – False; Tim Tebow holds the first-sophomore distinction.
339) Les Horvath
340) 1944
341) Troy Smith
342) Three, Bob Ferguson, 1961; John Hicks, 1973; and Keith Byars 1984

343) Who holds Ohio State's record for the most TD passes in a single season?

344) He threw 35 TD passes in 2006 to set the mark.

A) True
B) False

345) How many interceptions did he throw that season?

346) Is Terrelle Pryor or Bobby Hoying No. 2 on the list for this category?

347) What season did the player listed No. 2 in the category set his single-season high?

348) How many TD passes did he complete that season?

Answers:

343) Troy Smith
344) B – False; 30
345) Six
346) Bobby Hoying
347) 1995
348) 29

349) The Buckeyes' record for the most rushing yards in a career is _________.

350) Who owns the team record in the category?

351) How many seasons did he don the Buckeyes' scarlet and gray?

352) Who holds the No. 2 spot in the category?

353) How many rushing yards did he gain?

354) Did he play more than, fewer than or the same number of seasons in Columbus as the No. 1 rusher?

Answers:

349) 5,589
350) Archie Griffin
351) Four
352) Eddie George
353) 3,768
354) The same number as; Four

355) Who owns Ohio State's record for the highest passing efficiency rating in a single game?

356) What was his passing efficiency rating that game?

357) Who owns Ohio State's record for the highest passing efficiency rating in a single season?

358) What was his passing efficiency rating that year?

359) Who owns Ohio State's career record for the highest passing efficiency?

360) What was his career passing efficiency rating?

Answers:

355) John Borton
356) 339.4; Washington State, 1952
357) Bobby Hoying
358) 163.4; 1995
359) Terrelle Pryor
360) 158.4

361) The Buckeyes' individual record for the most rushing attempts in a game was set at Northwestern.

A) True
B) False

362) When was the record set?

363) Who set the record?

364) How many rushing attempts did he have?

365) How many yards did he gain that day?

366) How many TDs did he score that day?

Answers:

361) A – True
362) 1972
363) Harold Henson
364) 44
365) 153
366) Four

367) What are the most 200-yard rushing games by a Buckeye in career?

368) How many times has this been accomplished?

369) Who owns this Buckeye record?

370) What seasons did he do it?

371) Did any other Buckeye running back have three or more 200-yard performances in their careers?

372) What two Buckeyes had two 200-yard rushing games in a single season?

Answers:

367) Five
368) Two
369) Eddie George
370) 1994 and 1995
371) No
372) Archie Griffin (1972 and 1973) and Chris Wells (2007)

373) What was Ohio State's record heading into the 1969 Rose Bowl?

374) How many All-Americans played on the 1968 Buckeye team?

375) Who was the Buckeyes' opponent in the 1969 Rose Bowl?

376) Who was named Rose Bowl Player of the Game that year?

A) Rex Kern
B) Jack Tatum
C) Jim Otis
D) Bruce Jankowski

377) What was the final score of the game?

378) The 1969 Rose Bowl was the first of ______ Rose Bowl matchups between head coaches Woody Hayes and John McKay.

Answers:

373) 9-0
374) 11
375) Southern Cal Trojans
376) A – Rex Kern
377) Ohio State 27, Southern Cal 16
378) Four

379) Ted Ginn, Jr. returned eight punts for touchdowns during his career at Ohio State.

A) True
B) False

380) Were his punt returns for touchdowns good enough to set the Buckeyes' record for the category?

381) Who holds the No. 2 spot on the Buckeyes' career list in the category?

382) How many career punt returns for TDs do they have?

383) There are ___ Buckeyes with two career punt returns to their credit.

384) Of those who scored two TDs on punt returns during their career, who was the most recent?

Answers:

379) B – False; Six
380) Yes
381) Jeff Graham and Garcia Lane
382) Three each
383) Five
384) David Boston; 1996-98

385) What year was the Buckeyes' record for the highest kickoff return average set?

386) Who set the record?

387) What was his kickoff return average that season?

388) Ted Ginn, Jr. holds the No. 2 spot on the list.

A) True
B) False

389) What is the second highest average on the list?

390) Jordan Hall is the most recent player to be added to the top-10 list for the category. He is ranked sixth with a _____ average in _____.

Answers:

385) 1965
386) Tom Barrington
387) 34.3
388) B – False; Howard Cassady
389) 31.3
390) 27.9, 2010

391) What is Ohio State's all-time record in overtime games?

392) When was overtime introduced in NCAA Division I football?

393) What year did Ohio State play its first-ever overtime game?

394) Who was the Buckeyes' opponent that day?

395) When was the last time Ohio State played an overtime game?

396) Who was their opponent and what was the outcome?

Answers:

391) 5-2
392) 1996
393) 2002
394) Illinois; Ohio State 23, Illinois 16 (1OT)
395) 2011
396) Purdue; Purdue 26, Ohio State 23 (1OT)

397) Who holds the Buckeyes' record for the most field goal attempts in a season?

A) Josh Huston
B) Tim Williams
C) Dan Stultz
D) Mike Nugent

398) What year did he set the team record for the category?

399) How many field goat attempts did he have?

400) Who is second on the Buckeyes' single-season list for the category?

401) How many field goal attempts did the No. 2 players have?

402) What year did they secure the No. 2 spot on the list?

Answers:

397) B – Tim Williams
398) 1992
399) 29
400) Josh Huston and Mike Nugent
401) 28
402) 2005 (Josh Huston) and 2002 (Mike Nugent)

403) "Hang on Sloopy" is OSU's and the State of Ohio's official state rock song.

A) True
B) False

404) Who wrote the song?

405) What year was it first recorded?

406) What year was it first played by the OSU marching band?

407) Which band member is credited with convincing the band director to play it?

408) Who was the song named for?

Answers:

403) A – True; Approved by the 1985 Ohio General Assembly
404) Bert Berns and Wes Farrell
405) 1964; The Vibrations, later in 1965 it was recorded by the McCoys
406) 1965
407) John Tatgenhorst
408) Dorothy Sloop, American Jazz Musician born in Steubenville, Ohio

409) Who was the Buckeyes' first-ever Academic All-American?

410) What year did he receive the honor?

411) Dave Foley is Ohio State's only three-time Academic All-American.

A) True
B) False

412) Who was Ohio State's most recent Academic All-American?

413) When did he earn the distinction?

414) How many Buckeyes have won the William V. Campbell Trophy, formerly known as the Vincent DePaul Draddy Trophy?

Answers:

409) John Borton
410) 1952
411) A – True; 1966-68
412) Brian Robiskie
413) 2007 and 2008
414) Two; Bobby Hoying, 1995 and Craig Krenzel, 2003

415) What is the Buckeyes' team record for the most yards gained rushing in a single game?

416) The record was set against _______________.

417) When was the record set?

418) What are the most rushing attempts by the team in a single game?

419) Against what team were they made?

420) What year did this take place?

Answers:

415) 718
416) Mt. Union
417) 1930
418) 84
419) Illinois
420) 1973

421) Is the Buckeyes' record for the most passing attempts in a game over or under 60?

422) Which Buckeyes QB had the most passing attempts in a single game?

423) Against which team was the record set?

A) Florida State
B) Indiana
C) Duke
D) Navy

424) How many pass completions did he have that day?

425) How many TD passes did he complete that day?

426) ___________ won the game.

Answers:

421) Under; 52
422) Art Schlichter
423) A – Florida State
424) 31
425) Two
426) Florida State; 36-27

427) Craig Krenzel and Scott McMullen were party to four games in which they both had 100 or more yards of passing.

A) True
B) False

428) Who was the Buckeyes' opposition the firs time this happened in 2002?

429) How many yards passing did they each have?

430) How many yards passing did they each have the following year at Indiana?

431) In 2003, who was the Buckeyes' opponent when they completed the hat trick?

432) How many yards passing did they each have in that game?

Answers:

427) B – False; Three
428) San Jose State
429) 241, Craig Krenzel; 114, Scott McMullen
430) 272, Craig Krenzel; 111, Scott McMullen
431) Michigan
432) 221, Craig Krenzel; 108, Scott McMullen

433) Who set the Buckeyes' record for the most consecutive field goals made?

434) How many consecutive field goals did he make?

435) Were his consecutive field goals made in a single season or over two seasons?

436) When were they kicked?

437) What is the record for the second-most consecutive field goals made in Buckeyes history?

438) ____________ holds the No. 2 spot on the list for this category.

Answers:

433) Mike Nugent
434) 24
435) Over two seasons
436) 2001-02
437) 15
438) Vlade Janakievski

439) Did Joe Germaine ever passed for over 3,000 yards in a season?

440) Is he ranked No. 1 on the Buckeyes' list for the most yards passing in a season?

441) What year was the team's record set?

442) What is the next highest number of yards passing he had in a season?

443) Was that good enough to capture the No. 2 spot on the Buckeyes' list for this category?

444) How many times does Bobby Hoying appear on the Buckeyes' top-10 list for this category?

Answers:

439) Yes; 3,300
440) Yes
441) 1998
442) 1,847
443) No; Bobby Hoying owns No. 2 with 3,269 yards.
444) Two; Nos. 2 and 7

445) What year did the Ten-Year War between Ohio State and Michigan begin?

446) Who won the rivalry game between the two schools the year the Ten-Year War began?

447) How many National Championships did Ohio State win during that 10-year period?

448) How many National Championships did Michigan win during that 10-year period?

449) How many times did Ohio State defeat Michigan from 1969-78?

450) During the Ten-Year War Ohio State captured two Heisman Trophies to Michigan's zero.

A) True
B) False

Answers:

445) 1969
446) Michigan
447) One; 1970
448) Zero
449) Four; 4-5-1
450) A – True; Archie Griffin, 1974 and 1975

451) _______________ holds the Buckeyes' career and season records for the most TDs on kickoff returns.

452) How many TDs on kickoff returns did he score in his career at Ohio State?

453) What seasons did he play for the Buckeyes?

454) Which season did he score two TDs on kickoff returns?

455) Have any other Buckeyes scored two TDs on kickoff returns in their careers?

456) Who was the most recent Buckeye to run a kickoff return for a TD?

Answers:

451) Lenny Willis
452) Two
453) 1974-75
454) 1974
455) Yes; Ted Ginn, Jr. and Dean Sensanbaugher; Co-holders of the career record in this category
456) Jordan Hall; 2010, Michigan

457) Derek Ross holds the Buckeyes' record for the most interception return yards in a season.

A) True
B) False

458) What year did he set the mark?

459) How many interception return yards did he have that season?

460) Did Gary Berry amass over or under 175 interception return yards in 1997?

461) What position does he hold on the leaders list for this category?

462) Kurt Coleman accumulated ______ interception return yards in 2009.

Answers:

457) A – True
458) 2001
459) 194
460) Under; 166
461) No. 2
462) 129; Currently third in the category

463) The Buckeyes' team record for the most first downs in a game is _____.

464) What year was the team record set?

465) Which opponent gave up those first downs?

466) What is the team record for the most first downs in a season?

467) What season did they set that mark?

468) Did the team also set their record for the most first downs per game that season?

Answers:

463) 39
464) 1935
465) Drake
466) 303
467) 1995
468) No; That record is 27.8, set in 1969.

469) Pete Johnson scored exactly 50 rushing touchdowns in his career at Ohio State.

A) True
B) False

470) What is his rank on the Buckeyes' career leaders list?

471) How many rushing touchdowns did Keith Byars score?

472) He is ranked _____ of all time.

473) Who holds the No. 3 spot on the list?

474) How many rushing touchdowns is he credited with?

Answers:

469) B – False; 56
470) No. 1
471) 46
472) No. 2
473) Eddie George
474) 44

475) What is the Buckeyes' all-time record in night games?

476) Per available records, what year was their first-ever night game (kickoff after 5:00 p.m.)?

477) Where was that game played?

478) The Trojans defeated the Buckeyes 17-0 to win that game.

A) True
B) False

479) When was the most recent season the Buckeyes played at least two night games?

480) When was the most recent season they did not play a night game?

Answers:

475) 36-19
476) 1959
477) at Southern Cal
478) A – True
479) 2011; at Miami (Fla.), at Nebraska and vs. Wisconsin
480) 1996

481) Which Buckeye has maintained the highest field goal percentage for a season?

A) Aaron Pettrey
B) Vlade Janakievski
C) Mike Nugent
D) Josh Huston

482) He set the Buckeyes' record in the category in ______.

483) What average did he carry that season?

484) Does he occupy three of the top-five spots in the category?

485) What is the second-highest field goal percentage in team history?

486) What is the third highest?

Answers:

481) C – Mike Nugent
482) 2002
483) .893
484) Yes; Nos. 1, 2 and 5
485) .889
486) .875; Aaron Pettrey, 2008

487) Which bowl game did the Buckeyes play in following the 1957 regular season?

488) Was Ohio State ranked No. 1 in both the AP and Coaches polls prior to the game?

489) Who was the Buckeyes' opponent in the game?

490) The opposition scored two times before the Buckeyes got on the board.

A) True
B) False

491) Who was named Rose Bowl Player of the Game?

492) What was the final score of the game?

Answers:

487) 1958 Rose Bowl
488) No; AP No. 2 and Coaches No. 1
489) Oregon Ducks
490) B – False; OSU scored first with a first-quarter TD
491) Jack Crabtree, Oregon QB
492) Oregon 7, Ohio State 10

493) What are the most points Ohio State has scored in a bowl game?

494) What bowl opponent allowed those points?

495) This took place in the 1987 Cotton Bowl.

A) True
B) False

496) What are the most points Ohio State has allowed in a bowl game?

497) What bowl opponent scored those points?

498) Did this take place in the 1973 Rose Bowl?

Answers:

493) 47
494) BYU
495) B – False; 1982 Holiday Bowl
496) 42
497) Southern Cal
498) Yes

499) What year was the Buckeyes' record for the most passes had intercepted set?

500) Which Buckeyes QB set the record that year?

501) How many interceptions did he throw?

502) Is Todd Boeckman ranked No. 2 in the category?

503) How many interceptions did the No. 2 ranked player throw?

504) What year did that occur?

Answers:

499) 1978
500) Art Schlichter
501) 21
502) No; Greg Frey
503) 16
504) 1990

505) Is the Buckeyes' team record for the fewest net yards gained under or over 50?

506) Against which team did the record-low take place?

507) The year was _____.

508) Did the Buckeyes also set their team record for the fewest yards per attempt during this game?

509) What was their yards per attempt that game?

510) By what popular name is this game known and what was the final score?

Answers:

505) Under; 27
506) Michigan
507) 1950
508) Yes
509) 0.6
510) Snow Bowl; Michigan 9, Ohio State 3

511) How many times have Buckeyes receivers had 200 or more yards receiving in a single game?

512) Who was the most recent Buckeye to exceed 200?

513) David Boston appears ____ times on the Buckeyes' top-10 list for the most yards receiving in a game.

514) Do any current Buckeyes receivers appear on the top-10 list?

515) Who is the second most recent Buckeye to appear on the top-10 list?

516) What year did he earn his spot on the list?

Answers:

511) Four
512) Santonio Holmes
513) Two
514) No
515) Ken-Yon Rambo; Nos. 9 and 10
516) 1999

517) Who were the Buckeyes' team captains in 2011?

518) Who were the Buckeyes' first-ever team captains?

519) How many captains were named in 2010?

520) How many seasons was James Laurinaitis named a team captain?

521) Was Archie Griffin a team captain in both his Heisman Trophy-winning seasons?

522) What season was Kirk Herbstreit OSU's team captain?

Answers:

517) No permanent team captains were named in 2011
518) Jesse L. Jones and Paul M. Lincoln
519) Six: Browning, Heyward, Homan, Rolle, Saine and Sanzenbacher
520) Two; 2007 and 2008
521) Yes; 1974 and 1975
522) 1992

523) Which Buckeye holds the team record for the most 200-yard rushing games in a season?

A) Chris Wells
B) Archie Griffin
C) Keith Byars
D) Eddie George

524) How many 200-yard rushing games did he have in a season?

525) What year did he accomplish this feat?

526) Who holds the No. 2 spot on the list?

527) How many 200-yard rushing games did he have to secure that spot?

528) He secured his spot on this list in the ______ season.

Answers:

523) D – Eddie George
524) Three
525) 1995
526) Chris Wells
527) Two
528) 2007

529) What year did TBDBITL first perform Script Ohio?

530) What formation does the band assume to begin Script Ohio?

A) Square
B) Revolving Block "O"
C) Three-D Box
D) Rotating Line

531) What year did Michigan's marching band make a script of the word "Ohio" across the field?

532) Did they do this in Ann Arbor or Columbus?

533) What song is played by the band throughout the Script Ohio performance?

534) Which band member traditionally dots the "i"?

Answers:

529) 1936
530) B – Revolving Block "O"
531) 1932
532) Columbus
533) Le Regiment de Sambre et Meuse
534) Sousaphone player

535) Who holds the Buckeyes' career record for the most punt attempts?

536) How many career punt attempts did he have at Ohio State?

537) How many seasons was he a Buckeye?

538) How many career punt attempts did the player in the No. 2 spot have?

539) Who is ranked second on the career list?

540) He played for the Buckeyes from 1984 to ______.

Answers:

535) Brent Bartholomew
536) 237
537) Four; 1995-98
538) 214
539) Tom Tupa
540) 1987

541) Who was the first Buckeye awarded the Lombardi Award?

542) What year did he receive the award?

543) The award is named for whom?

544) What does the award recognize?

A) Best on-field leader
B) Best cornerback
C) Best safety
D) Best lineman or linebacker

545) Has any Buckeye ever won the award twice?

546) Who was the most recent Buckeye to win the award?

Answers:

541) Jim Stillwagon
542) 1970
543) Vince Lombardi
544) D – Best lineman or linebacker
545) Yes; Orlando Pace
546) A.J. Hawk

547) What was the first-ever bowl game Ohio State played in?

548) What was the name of the game at the time?

549) Who was the Buckeyes' opponent that day?

550) Was Ohio State victorious that day?

551) What was the final margin of loss for the Buckeyes?

552) Was this Ohio State's only loss of the season?

Answers:

547) 1921 Rose Bowl
548) Tournament East-West Football Game
549) Cal Golden Bears
550) No
551) 28 points; Cal 28, Ohio State 0
552) Yes

553) Fred Bruney is the original holder of the Buckeyes' record for the most interceptions in a game.

A) True
B) False

554) How many interceptions did he make in a game to set the record?

555) When was the record first set?

556) Did he match his own feat in a game the following year?

557) Against what team did he match his own record?

558) Who is the most recent Buckeye to tie the record?

Answers:

553) A – True; Co-holder with seven other Buckeyes
554) Three; Nine times this has happened.
555) 1951
556) Yes
557) Michigan
558) Damon Moore; 1996 at Iowa

559) What is the Buckeyes' career record for the highest punt return average?

560) Who holds the record?

561) When did he set the record?

562) Who is ranked No. 2?

563) What was his career punt return average?

564) How many seasons did he spend in Ohio State?

Answers:

559) 14.3
560) Neal Colzie
561) 1972-74
562) Ted Ginn, Jr.
563) 14.1
564) Three

565) What is the record for the longest rushing play against the Buckeyes by an opponent?

566) Who set this record and what year did he do it?

567) What team did he play for?

568) What is the second longest rushing play allowed by Ohio State?

569) Levi Jackson of ________________ is credited with this rushing play.

570) Did O.J. Simpson have an 85-yard rushing play against Ohio State in the Rose Bowl?

Answers:

565) 91 yards
566) Larry Ferguson; 1960
567) Iowa
568) 88 yards
569) Michigan State
570) No; 80-yard rush; Tied for third longest against OSU

571) What is the Buckeyes' team record for the most sacks in a game?

572) Which opponent allowed the sacks?

573) What year did this take place?

574) ___________ was MSU's quarterback that day.

575) How many yards in losses resulted from the record-setting number of sacks?

576) Which Buckeye defender logged the most sacks on the day?

A) Bobby Carpenter
B) A.J. Hawk
C) David Patterson
D) Mike Kudla

Answers:

571) 12
572) Michigan State
573) 2005
574) Drew Stanton
575) 58
576) A – Bobby Carpenter

577) Who holds the Buckeyes' record for the most yards rushing in a season?

A) Archie Griffin
B) Keith Byars
C) Eddie George
D) Chris Wells

578) He set the record in ______.

579) How many yards rushing did he have that year?

580) Did he play all 13 games for the Buckeyes that season?

581) How many rushing attempts did he have?

582) How many TDs did he score that year?

Answers:

577) C – Eddie George
578) 1995
579) 1,927
580) Yes
581) 328
582) 24

583) Jim Tressel was named head coach of the Ohio State Buckeyes in 2001.

A) True
B) False

584) How many seasons did Tressel spend as the Buckeyes head coach?

585) Tressel coached the Buckeyes to how many undefeated regular seasons?

586) What was his record against Michigan?

587) What was his record in bowl games?

588) What was his overall record?

Answers:

583) A – True
584) 10
585) Two; 2002 and 2006
586) 9-1
587) 6-4
588) 106-22

589) How many times did Joe Germaine pass for 300 or more yards in a game?

590) Does he hold the Buckeyes' record for the category?

591) Germaine has more than twice as many 300-yard passing games as the Buckeye QB with the second most.

A) True
B) False

592) What were the most yards passing by Germaine in a single game?

593) This is the _____-most in Buckeyes history.

594) Does Greg Frey or Bobby Hoying hold the No. 3 spot?

Answers:

589) Eight
590) No; Art Schlichter, 458 yards vs. Florida State, 1981
591) A – True; Troy Smith and Art Schlichter each have three
592) 378
593) Second
594) Greg Frey; 362 yards at Minnesota, 1989

595) All time, how many conference titles has Ohio State won?

596) What year did Ohio State join the Big Ten?

597) When was the first year Ohio State won a Big Ten title?

598) What are the most consecutive years Ohio State won or shared the Big Ten title?

599) In the ten year period from 2001 to 2010, Ohio State won ______ Big Ten titles.

600) Is this the Big Ten record for the most titles in a 10-year span?

Answers:

595) 36; 2 OAC and 34 Big Ten (Excludes vacated season)
596) 1913
597) 1916
598) Six; 1972-77
599) Six (Excludes vacated season)
600) No; Ohio State had nine from 1968-77 to set the record.

601) What is Ohio State's team record for the most consecutive bowl appearances?

A) 9
B) 11
C) 14
D) 15

602) What year did the streak begin?

603) Did the Buckeyes win or lose the first game in the streak?

604) Ohio State had a ________ win-loss record during the streak.

605) Did the Buckeyes win or lose the final game of the streak?

606) Who did they defeat in the final game of the bowl appearance streak?

Answers:

601) D – 15
602) 1972
603) Lose
604) 7-8
605) Win
606) Texas A&M; 28-12, Cotton Bowl

607) What is Ohio State's team record for the most forced fumbles in a season?

A) 40
B) 46
C) 50
D) 56

608) What year was this team record established?

609) How many of these fumbles did the Buckeyes recover?

610) In the ______ season, Ohio State set its team record for the most forced fumbles recovered.

611) How many forced fumbles did the Buckeyes recover that season?

612) How many fumbles did the Buckeyes force that season?

Answers:

607) B – 46
608) 1957
609) 24
610) 1950
611) 25
612) 43

613) The Buckeyes' team record for the most yards gained passing in a single game is _______.

614) Was this game played at home or away?

615) Which of these teams gave up the passing yards?

A) Penn State
B) Washington State
C) Florida State
D) Michigan State

616) Who was the Buckeyes' quarterback that record-setting day?

617) What were the teams ranked heading into the game?

618) Did Ohio State emerge victorious that day?

Answers:

613) 459
614) Away
615) A – Penn State
616) Stanley Jackson and Joe Germaine
617) Ohio State No. 7 and Penn State No. 2
618) No; Ohio State 27, Penn State 31

619) Where is Ohio State QB Braxton Miller from?

620) How many yards passing did Miller have in 2011?

621) Did Miller have less than or more than 15 passing TDs in 2011?

622) How many rushing TDs did he have in 2011?

623) What was his pass efficiency rating in 2011?

624) Was Miller named the Big Ten Freshman of the Year in 2011?

Answers:

619) Huber Heights, Ohio
620) 1,159
621) Less than; 13
622) Seven
623) 138.4
624) Yes

625) What is the name of Ohio State's costumed mascot?

A) Bobby Buckeye
B) Bucky Buckeye
C) Brutus Buckeye
D) Benny Buckeye

626) He made his debut in 1965.

A) True
B) False

627) Who was the Buckeyes' opponent for his first game?

628) He once appeared in ESPN's This is SportsCenter ads exercising with __________.

629) What jersey number does he wear?

630) What year did he enter the Mascot Hall of Fame?

Answers:

625) C – Brutus Buckeye
626) A – True
627) Minnesota
628) Richard Simmons and ESPN staff
629) No. 00
630) 2007

631) When were the first trees planted at Buckeye Grove?

632) How many trees were planted that year?

633) What did the first trees planted represent?

A) The first All-Conference players
B) The donors who made the grove possible
C) The first years of OSU football
D) The first starters of the OSU football team

634) What was the original name of Buckeye Grove?

635) For whom are trees planted?

636) How many trees are currently planted in Buckeye Grove?

Answers:

631) 1929
632) 11
633) D – The first starters of the OSU football team
634) Buckeye All-American Arbor
635) Football Buckeye All-Americans
636) 134

637) Who was the Buckeyes' team MVP for the 1930 season?

638) What position did he play?

639) He was also named Big Ten MVP that year.

A) True
B) False

640) In what classic photo was he famously depicted?

641) Who took the photo?

642) Where is the photo on display?

Answers:

637) Wes Fesler
638) End
639) A – True
640) "Wes Fesler Kicking a Football"
641) Doc Edgerton
642) The Metropolitan Museum of Art, New York

643) How many Buckeyes have earned All-American selections three times in their careers?

644) Chic Harley earned his third selection in which year?

645) Wes Fesler was named All-American for the third time in _____.

646) Archie Griffin earned his third All-American selection in 1976.

A) True
B) False

647) Did Tom Skladany earn his third All-American selection in 1977?

648) Was James Laurinaitis the most recent Buckeye to become a three-time All-American?

Answers:

643) Eight
644) 1919
645) 1930
646) B – False; 1975
647) No; 1976
648) Yes; 2006-08

649) What is the Buckeyes' record for the most yards on kickoff returns in a career?

650) Which Buckeye set this team record?

651) How many seasons did he spend at Ohio State?

652) ______ was his last season in the scarlet and gray.

653) How many kickoff returns attempts did he have in his career with the Buckeyes?

654) Who is second on the Buckeyes' career list for this category?

A) Carlos Snow
B) Howard Cassady
C) Ken-Yon Rambo
D) Ted Ginn, Jr.

Answers:

649) 1,642
650) Maurice Hall
651) Four
652) 2004
653) 72
654) C – Ken-Yon Rambo; 1,410

655) What is the record attendance for a game at Ohio Stadium?

656) Was it a day or night game?

657) This record was set in ______.

658) Who was the Buckeyes' opponent that game?

659) Was the record crowd treated to a Buckeyes victory?

660) What was the contest's final score?

Answers:

655) 106,033
656) Night game
657) 2009
658) Southern Cal
659) No
660) USC 18, Ohio State 15

661) Terry Glenn owns the Buckeyes' record for the highest average yards per catch in a season.

A) True
B) False

662) What is the record for this category?

663) What year was the record set?

664) Who holds the No. 2 spot on the list?

665) What was the No. 2 player's average yards per catch for the season?

666) Who sits in the No. 3 spot and what was his season average?

Answers:

661) B – False; Cedric Anderson
662) 27.6
663) 1982
664) Brian Hartline
665) 22.8; 2008
666) Terry Glenn, 22.0; 1995

667) How many games did Terrelle Pryor start his freshman season?

668) He had a ______ win-loss record that year.

669) How many starts did he have his sophomore season?

670) What was his record that year?

671) Did he have an equal number of starts in his junior year as his sophomore year?

672) He won one more game in his junior year than in his sophomore year.

A) True
B) False

Answers:

667) Nine
668) 8-1
669) 13
670) 11-2
671) Yes
672) A – True; 12-1

673) What is Ohio State's record for the most touchdowns responsible for in a season?

674) How many Buckeyes QBs co-hold this record?

675) ____________ is the most recent to tie the record.

676) Who is the second-most recent QB to place his name in the No. 1 spot on the list?

677) What year did he add his name?

678) Who is the remaining QB and what year did he achieve the mark?

Answers:

673) 31
674) Three
675) Terrelle Pryor
676) Troy Smith
677) 2006
678) Bobby Hoying, 1995

679) What year was the Buckeyes' record for the most yards on punt returns in a season set?

A) 1971
B) 1973
C) 1975
D) 1977

680) Who set the record that season?

681) He had _____ punt return yards that year.

682) Who sits in the No. 2 spot on the Buckeyes' list for the category?

683) How many punt return yards did he amass to earn his No. 2 ranking?

684) What year did the No. 2 man earn his spot?

Answers:

679) B – 1973
680) Neal Colzie
681) 679
682) Nate Clements
683) 513
684) 2000

685) Mike Nugent holds the Buckeyes' career record for the most field goals made.

A) True
B) False

686) Does he have two times as many career field goals as Dan Stultz?

687) __________ sits in the No. 3 spot on the Buckeyes' career list for the most field goals.

688) How many field goals did he make?

689) Is Vlade Janakievski ranked in the top five on this list?

690) How many career field goals did he make?

Answers:

685) A – True; 72
686) No; 72 to 59
687) Tim Williams
688) 49
689) Yes
690) 41

691) In 1979, ____________ set the Buckeyes' record for the longest pass play.

692) Who received the pass on the play?

693) How many yards did the play go?

694) How many other Buckeyes quarterback-receiver combinations have gone 80 yards or more on a pass play?

695) When did the most recent 80-plus yard pass play take place?

696) What passer-receiver combination did this, and what ranking do they have on this list?

Answers:

691) Art Schlichter
692) Calvin Murray
693) 86
694) Five
695) 2005
696) Troy Smith and Santonio Holmes, No. 2

697) The most completed passes by a Buckeyes QB in a game are _____.

698) Against which teams was this record set?

699) Which Buckeye quarterbacks share the record?

700) What year did the games take place?

701) Who holds the No. 3 spot on this list?

A) Troy Smith and Joe Germaine
B) Kirk Herbstreit and Greg Frey
C) Craig Krenzel and Mike Tomczak
D) John Borton and Bobby Hoying

702) How many passes did they complete in a single game to capture the No. 3 spot?

Answers:

697) 31
698) Indiana and Florida State
699) Joe Germaine and Art Schlichter
700) 1998 (at Indiana) and 1981 (Florida State)
701) A – Troy Smith and Joe Germaine
702) 29

703) Where was Urban Meyer's place of birth?

704) Where did he attend college?

705) What year was he drafted?

706) He played quarterback for the Bearcats.

A) True
B) False

707) What year did he coach his first game as a head coach?

708) Did he ever coach at the high school level?

Answers:

703) Toledo, Ohio
704) Cincinnati
705) Not drafted
706) B – False; Defensive back
707) 2001
708) Yes; St. Xavier High School, Ohio; DB coach

709) Since 1960, what is Ohio State's team record for the most offense attempts in a game?

710) This record was set in a game against Oregon.

A) True
B) False

711) What year was the record set?

712) Prior to 1960, what was Ohio State's team record for the most offense attempts in a game?

713) Against what team was the record set?

714) What year did this take place?

Answers:

709) 101
710) B – False; Illinois
711) 1969
712) 101
713) Texas Christian
714) 1927

715) What is Ohio State's all-time record when ranked No. 1?

716) Ohio State is ______ when their opponent is ranked No. 1.

717) What is the Buckeyes' all-time record when ranked in the top 10?

718) What is Ohio State's all-time record when both they and their opponent are ranked?

719) What is Ohio State's all-time record when their opponent is ranked in the top 10?

720) The last time Ohio State played in a No.1-versus-No. 2 matchup was in the 2008 BCS National Championship game.

A) True
B) False

Answers:

715) 66-11-1
716) 4-9
717) 314-76-9
718) 115-85-10
719) 67-51-8
720) A – True; No. 1 Ohio State vs. No. 2 LSU